Why Ostriches Don't Fly

and

Other Tales from the African Bush

WORLD FOLKLORE SERIES

1991   *Folk Stories of the Hmong: Peoples of Laos, Thailand, and Vietnam.* By Norma J. Livo and Dia Cha.

1992   *Images of a People: Tlingit Myths and Legends.* By Mary Helen Pelton and Jacqueline DiGennaro.

1994   *Hyena and the Moon: Stories to Tell from Kenya.* By Heather McNeil.

1994   *The Corn Woman: Stories and Legends of the Hispanic Southwest.* Retold by Angel Vigil. Translated by Juan Francisco Marín and Jennnifer Audrey Lowell.

1994   *Thai Tales: Folktales of Thailand.* Retold by Supaporn Vathanaprida. Edited by Margaret Read MacDonald.

1996   *In Days Gone By: Folklore and Traditions of the Pennsylvania Dutch.* By Audrey Burie Kirchner and Margaret R. Tassia.

1997   *Why Ostriches Don't Fly and Other Tales from the African Bush.* By I. Murphy Lewis.

1997   *From the Mango Tree and Other Folktales from Nepal.* By Kavita Ram Shrestha and Sarah Lamstein.

Selections Available on Audiocassette

1995   *Hyena and the Moon: Stories to Listen to from Kenya.* By Heather McNeil.

1995   *The Corn Woman: Audio Stories and Legends of the Hispanic Southwest.* English and Spanish versions. By Angel Vigil. Spanish version read by Juan Francisco Marín.

Why Ostriches Don't Fly

and

Other Tales from the African Bush

I. Murphy Lewis
Illustrated by the Author

Foreword by Izak Barnard

1997

LIBRARIES UNLIMITED, INC.
Englewood, Colorado

LIBRARIES UNLIMITED, INC.
P.O. Box 6633
Englewood, CO 80155-6633
1-800-237-6124

Project Editor: Constance Hardesty
Interior Design and Typesetting: Judy Gay Matthews

Library of Congress Cataloging-in-Publication Data

Lewis, Irene Murphy, 1958-
   Why ostriches don't fly and other tales from the African bush /
I. Murphy Lewis ; illustrated by the author.
   xxxii, 113 p. 19x26 cm.
   Includes bibliographical references.
   ISBN 1-56308-402-3
   1. San (African people)--Folklore. 2. San (African people)--
Social life and customs. 3. Tales--Kalahari Desert. 4. Kalahari
Desert--Social life and customs. I. Title.
GR358.2.B83L48   1996
398'.089961--dc20

                                     96-27980
                                         CIP

Foreword

The Kalahari—to know its various life forms, from small, seemingly insignificant insects to highly complex ecosystems, has been my privilege during the last thirty some odd years of my life. The masters of this thirstland, my friends the Bushmen, came from hazy primeval times to survive in today's bewildering modern world . . . without a written language.

Through the skillful pen of Murphy Lewis this ancient culture speaks to you about their past, their present, and their future. The way in which she does this confirms her thorough research, first-hand knowledge, and sensitive intuition. Read carefully between the lines and you will experience part of your own origin and roots.

Izak Barnard

Dedication

To Izak Barnard, explorer, farmer:
For his technical advice.
For the hours spent educating me with map
and pointer in hand.
For the divine conversations around the campfire at each night's feast,
sky lit by the Southern Cross, table lit by candles,
as Mantis looked on.
For his boldness in taking three Kansans into the Kalahari
with no gun, no radio, no fear.

To my parents, Janet and Ted Lewis:
For walking the razor's edge with me daily,
even to the extreme of bumping along in a rebuilt
1971 International truck on Safari in the Kalahari.

To my friends, A. Gail Segal, Lyndy Simons,
Dr. Brooke Sarno-Royse:
For their support, wisdom, insight, and many hours spent
reading and editing this manuscript.

To my NYC family,
Brigitte Moody and her dog, Bojangles:
For homecooked meals, long walks and talks,
and fights with Bo over his famous carrot, in a vast and lonely city.

To Barbara Seuling, writer, teacher:
For first believing in my work.

To Laurens van der Post, author, explorer:
For opening my eyes to the beauty of the Bushmen, to their plight.
For introducing me to their stories
that I might share them with children,
and for encouraging me in this endeavor.

To Johannes Vahrmeijer, botanist, explorer:
For intelligently and gently saving my face
with his brilliant botanical skills.

To Charles Cornwall, Eva Monley, David Coulson,
Alec Campbell, and Tim Liversidge:
Though I barely know them, for their faxes, generosity, kindness,
and insight in leading me to a successful safari.

Contents

Contents

Preface

Five years ago, my dear friend Gail Segal gave me a magnificent book, *The Mantis Carol*, by Sir Laurens van der Post, and with it, a whole new world. I was so captivated by Hans Taaibosch, the Bushman van der Post wrote about, that I voraciously devoured every book of his I could find.

As I read his books, it occurred to me how beautiful are the tales of the Bushmen—and how important it is for the children of the world to read them. And so I began correspondence with Sir Laurens to bring this about. On my first visit to London, in the fall of 1994, I had the marvelous opportunity to meet with him, to receive his advice and blessing. My dream began to come true.

Of course, a visit to Africa was a must. My parents—the Lord bless them—decided to join me. In August of 1995, with a four-man crew from Penduka Safaris, we drove two days into the Kalahari Desert of Botswana to see the Bushmen at Molapo. Another dream had come true.

In April of 1996, I went back to the Kalahari Desert along with Izak Barnard and his friend, Johannes Vahrmeijer, to meet the Bushmen at Phuduhudu. There I had the opportunity to meet two of the artists whose work has appeared at the Louvre. They drew for me and told me 22 tales I had never heard. Other Bushmen took us gathering for food in the veld and taught us how to make a fire and bow and arrows. At night, as the sun set majestically, they danced and sang for us.

The following pages are my attempt to share their world through my illustrations, photographs, and some of the tales they gave to me. I hope they will touch you as they have me.

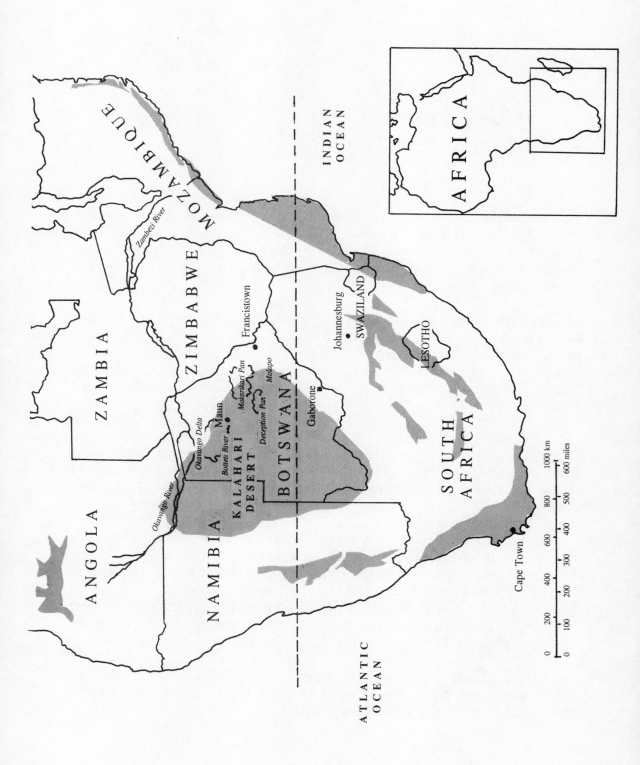

A Gentle People in the Thirstland

Today, deep in the heart of southern Africa, the ancient nomadic tribe of the Bushmen travel and hunt throughout the Kalahari Desert, "the place that dried up long ago." Years before, they roamed the northern territories of Africa and the Mediterranean before the coming of Egyptians, Phoenicians, Carthaginians, Greeks, and Romans. In the Second Dynasty of Egypt, the Bushman's unique human physique was described in the hieroglyphic records. Now, there is no trace of them in the north. Only in the Kalahari Desert, an area that covers most of Botswana and parts of Namibia, Angola and South Africa a mere handful of the race remains.

Storytelling.

A South African officer, Charles Cornwall, who served with several Bushmen in the early 1980s during the war between the Namibian independence movement, SWAPO, and the South African army, found the Bushmen to be a remarkable people. Cornwall observed their superb skills at tracking both game and enemy.

Most notably, Cornwall spoke of their astonishing memory. Without knowledge of mechanics, they could disassemble an automobile and perfectly reassemble the vehicle piece by piece. While tracking in the middle of the desert, the Bushmen could find a waterhole they had not used in months. At night, around the campfire and under the wide African sky, they told spendid tales from childhood with total recall.

The Bushmen have always been known for their storytelling. It appears to be the supreme expression of their spirit. Perhaps they know that, without a story, there could be no nation, no culture, no civilization, no life. When I asked about this, they replied, "We have a dream dreaming us."

This book provides a glimpse of the history of the Bushmen; their hunting–gathering lifestyle, the changes they face today, and the stories they tell of animals, creation, and their gods.

Storytelling.

The Harmless People: The Bushmen and Their Culture

Many anthropologists and photographers have gone into the desert to study the Bushmen. Elizabeth Marshall Thomas, author of *The Harmless People*, traveled and lived among the Bushmen for a year in the late 1950s. During this time, Thomas observed their nature and began to understand why the race has diminished so quickly over the last century.

She found them to be quite submissive. It is not in their spirit to fight unless it is to defend the land, the water, and the animals they believe to be theirs, as they did against the *trekkers*, or pioneers, in the late 1600s. If a problem should arise, they would much rather run away until the problem passes. Unlike the neighboring tribe of Bantu, cattlemen known for their bravery in battle, the Bushmen deplore bravery. In their mythological tales, the hero is the one who plays tricks or tells lies, as Pishiboro does in "Where Are All the Big Feet?" To the Bushmen, the mighty lion, for example, wields power but is not as wise as their favored bird, the ostrich, who defeats the lion with wisdom in the story "Who Is the Greatest of Them All?"

The Bushmen are completely overwhelmed by the wealth of goods among the Bantu and Europeans. The Bushmen find these peoples to be enormous and powerful, beyond imagination, possessing many things, and therefore superior. The Bushmen have names for these strangers: *zhu dole*, or dangerous person, and *zo si*, or animals without hooves. They feel these people are to be avoided like angry lions and hyenas.

But the real problem lies in the fact that the Bantu and Europeans see the Bushmen as inferior. The result has been the breakdown of a submissive race, *zhu twa si*, as the !Kung Bushmen call themselves, the harmless people.

At Home in the Thirstland

The Bushmen have long been regarded as the earliest human inhabitants in southern Africa. Scattered across the land, their relics of rock paintings, rock engravings, and stone implements are the oldest records of human habitation to be found.

Yet, centuries ago, the Bushmen's isolated range was invaded by cattlemen from the north. Then, in the late 1600s, trekkers from Europe, landing at Cape Town to seek their fortune in Africa, invaded them from the south. Many Bushmen died trying to defend their land. Eventually, only a remnant of the race remained, in the thirstland of the Kalahari Desert.

The Kalahari is so dry that many of the Bushmen's songs and dances are about the hope of coming rains. The women cry out and sing:

Under the sun
The earth is dry.
By the fire,
Alone I cry.
All day long
The earth cries
For the rain to come.
All night my heart cries
For my hunter to come
And take me away.

—*The Heart of the Hunter*, Laurens van der Post

Though covered with sand, the Kalahari is different from other deserts. The plain is also covered with tough, sun-bleached grasses; albizzia trees; *Raasblaar,* or the noisy apple-leaf trees; various flowering acacia trees; and bushes. In the Kalahari Game Reserve, one will find many creatures; steenboks, yellowbilled hornbills, jackals, goshawks, gemsboks, springboks, lappet-faced vultures, kudu, ostriches, black korhaans, praying mantis, scorpions, and cheetahs.

Kudu hiding in bush at Okavango Delta.

In the Kalahari, 3,000 feet above sea level, the most delightful season is winter. At this time of year, a smell like sage permeates the desert, and the rhythm of the gecko echoes throughout the plain. During the other seasons, the heat is oppressive during the day, but when the sun goes down, the sand cools and the temperature can become extremely cold.

The arid Kalahari is scored with *omurambas*, ancient river beds, and *salt pans*, ancient lakes or ponds that are hard as rock. In good times, there are a few *sip wells*, or water holes, scattered throughout the Kalahari. The average rainfall is 16–18 inches, the bulk of this rain falling in the summer. The only running water is concentrated in the north, in the Okavango Delta, located in the Moremi Reserve. (In 1963, this reserve was established by the Tawana people of the Maun region. It was one of the first reserves in Africa proclaimed by a local tribe. Today, the Department of Wildlife and National Parks oversees its operation.) Occasionally its reed-choked swamp overflows into the Botteti River, its waters reaching as far as Orapa or the Makarikari Pans.

Lappet-faced vultures.

The Harmless People: The Bushmen and Their Culture

Naturally, the water attracts a large amount of game: impalas; water buffaloes; lions; hippopotami; wildebeests; zebras; giraffes; red lechwes; crocodiles; and lovely birds: egrets, African darters, and fish eagles. The Moremi Reserve is covered with a forest of mopane trees. The mopane leaf is a favorite treat of the elephant. (The leaf resembles the elephant ear!) Because of this, large breeding herds are found in the Moremi Reserve.

Mopane leaf.

Still, in the deepest part of the Kalahari, little water can be found. In the distance, as the Bushman waits for rain and hears the cry of his woman, he can be heard singing his reply:

> *Oh! listen to the wind,*
> *You woman there;*
> *The time is coming,*
> *The rain is near.*
> *Listen to your heart,*
> *Your hunter is here.*

> —*The Heart of the Hunter*, Laurens van der Post

A Gentle People in the Thirstland

Elephants on the march!

The *Khoisan* People

Khoisan is the name that denotes the racial stock of two groups of people, the Bushmen and the Hottentots. The term comes from *Khoi-Khoin*, the name the Hottentots called themselves, and *San*, the name the Hottentots called the Bushmen. The Bushmen have no collective name of their own. Today, most African tribes call them the Bushpeople, or *Basarwa.*

The Bushmen and Hottentots were given the name *Khoisan* because they were similar in race, language, religion, and culture. Among the many differences between the two tribes, the most significant was that the Hottentots were pastoral people who kept sheep and cattle and lived in large, complex communities. The Bushmen lived in small, nomadic groups and subsisted on hunting and gathering, occasionally tending goats.

Physical Characteristics

Tshjamm: Good day! I heard
you coming from afar and, hearing,
felt myself live again so that
I came hurrying to meet you.

—Bushman greeting

Perhaps one of the most interesting characteristics of the Bushmen is the way they perceive themselves physically. In paintings all across Africa, the Bushmen have drawn themselves as tall as the giants (that is, the Bantu and Europeans) surrounding them. Yet, historically, the average height of a Bushman is five feet.

In *The Heart of the Hunter*, Laurens van der Post suggests the Bushmen's stature greatly worries them, and one should never mention it. Nor should one be shocked when coming upon a Bushman in the bush, because this would surely imply that he is ever so small. If surprised, one must immediately say to the Bushman, "Please do not look so offended. Do you really imagine a big person like you could hide without being seen? Why we saw you from a long way off and came straight here!" With this response one is sure to get a warm welcome. Or, one could offer the greeting, "Tshjamm!"

Other racial characteristics that make the Bushmen unique are yellow-brown skin; tight, spiral-tufted hair like peppercorns; and slanted eyes. In a good hunting season, when there is plenty to eat and drink, the Bushmen's stomach and buttocks protrude. The buttocks become so large, it is said one could set a glass of water on them, as if on a shelf. The Bushmen's skin is loose, and early in life becomes greatly wrinkled.

The most unique physical characteristic of the Bushmen is their intimate parts. The women are born with a natural apron over their genitals called *tablier egyptien*, and the men are born, live, and die with their sexual organ in a semi-erect position. The male Bushman declares this uniqueness with a name he has given himself, *qhwai-xkhwe*. Their rock paintings show this uniqueness.

Hunter–Gatherers

*Take away my aim which
is so poor because it is
human and give me the aim
of a star which never errs.*

—A hunter's prayer to a star

Three hunters.

At the beginning of the twentieth century, only 163 societies scattered throughout the world were said to be *hunter–gatherer* societies. The Bushmen were grouped in this category because they lived virtually independently as *nomads* subsisting on wild plants and animals. Today, there are very few hunter–gatherer societies left, including the true nomadic Bushmen.

Anthropologists have always been fascinated by these hunter–gatherer societies because they live on a *low-energy budget* and seem to keep their *ecosystems* at equilibrium. The Bushmen are known to be extremely self-sufficient; literally everything they require for survival can be found in their home range.

The Harmless People: The Bushmen and Their Culture

Bow and arrows.

The men have always dominated the hunt. Two to three times a week they venture forth to hunt or trap antelopes, spring hares, tortoises, and smaller animals. The men travel in pairs or small groups, for they cannot afford to miss their prey. They work well as a team, tracking the *spoor* of an animal. When not involved in the hunt, they are busy preparing poison for their arrows from the cocoons of certain beetles, repairing or making weapons, or recounting their experiences. The Bushmen never kill more than they need for survival.

While the men hunt, the women make other basic provisions. Daily, they and the children gather firewood and food. They set off on their expedition into the *veld*, or grassland, armed with digging sticks; ostrich eggs filled with drinking water; and *karosses*, or bags made from the hide of an animal, to carry the pickings of the day. The women, with their children as apprentices, search for *veldkos*, food from the veld, such as melons, roots, tubers, nuts, and berries. Many times there is no meat from the hunt. For weeks the Bushmen may subsist on a vegetarian diet.

Woman gathers wood.

Bands

There are many tribes of Bushmen scattered throughout the Kalahari: the !Kung, the Gikwe, the Kwa, the Deti, the Gxannakwe, and the Ju/'hoansi, to name a few. They travel in bands or small family groups of only 20–50 people. Rarely does the band become large, unless it is in a season of plenty when water and food can be easily obtained.

When they find a place to build their *werf*, or camp, the head of the tribe starts the first fire. To the Bushmen, fire is sacred. The flame for each *scherm*, or hut, is started from the leader's fire. Their fires never cease; the burning coals are tended until the group moves to the next werf.

Most of their work is completed in the morning. In the heat of the afternoon, everyone either comes together at the campsite to rest under the shade of a sparse tree or rests in the cool of their own hut. Children play, sing, or dance in groups. Someone may even play a tune on the *setinkane*, or thumb piano, and the *//gwashi*, or the five-stringed musical instrument made from the heartwood of the male mangetti tree.

The Bushmen choose to work out their differences. They tend to be very verbal and forthright, discussing issues and problems as a group. They know fighting could bring instant death, for their only weapon, the poison arrow, has no antidote. One cut on the arm would mean instant death. This could mean the loss of a great hunter or tracker, and therefore, starvation for all.

The community works cooperatively. Each day's kill or collected food is shared. The Bushmen cannot afford to be selfish or fight, for they are interdependent. They prefer peace. To the Bushmen, possessions, like a fine knife, can only cause jealousy and envy. They quickly use such possessions and pass them on. The only possessions they want are those they can carry on their back.

Children at play.

Language

The Bushmen speak one of the most phonetically complex languages in the world. The language has the distinctive feature of clicking and popping sounds. The lateral click is much like the sound cowboys use to spur on a horse. Another click reminds one of the English expression of annoyance, "tsk, tsk."

The German scholar Dr. Wilhelm H. I. Bleek and his sister-in-law, Dr. Lucy C. Lloyd, lived among the Cape Bushmen in the second half of the nineteenth century. They were the first to make an intensive study to record the Bushmen's language and their stories and translate them into English.

According to Izak Barnard, even before the other tribes of Africa had words for gold, copper, silver and iron, the Bushmen had these words in their vocabulary. In 1681, according to official accounts of that time, copper was brought to the Cape Colony from mines in the western Cape Province. The only people living in the area at that time were the Bushmen. Although hunter–gatherers, they were mining these ores and making tools as well. They traded these four minerals, along with ivory, with the pastoral black people of South Africa. This occasional exchange allowed the Bushmen to obtain essential commodities. R. J. Mason, in his journal *Background to the Transvaal Iron Age*, wrote that Bushmen skeletons were found in the deeper mines in western Zimbabwe and eastern Botswana.

Music and Dance

Many nights, the Bushmen fill the darkness with a roaring fire and rhythmic dance. The men dress in costumes to mimic their favorite animals. To resemble Mantis, long walking sticks are used. The biggest celebration comes after they catch the favored antelope, the eland. Dressed in the eland's skin, the men dance all night until they collapse by the fire from exhaustion.

Sometimes the men dance for fire, calling to the moon to send fire to the earth. (In this,

Antelope (eland) dance.

they are dancing for fire in the large, mythical sense.) The women clap, sing, and taunt the men for not finding the fire. In search of it, the men may even eat coals or throw themselves into the fire. When the mythic fire is found, they believe, rain will come.

The children love to mock the footsteps of their parents. The cocoons of a hairy caterpillar are filled with stones and seeds to make rattling bracelets tied around their ankles. These bracelets shake to the rhythmn of their steps.

One of their favorite dances is The Ostrich. The children face one another and begin to shuffle their feet together in the sand. One

crouches or bends over double from the hip. Another dancer, "the ostrich," swings his leg over the first boy's back

Praying mantis dance.

without missing a beat. All the while their movement is accompanied by a spoken rhythmic sound: "he he hi ... hehe he hi." It is a fast and vigorous game. One must be extremely coordinated to dance, sing, and slap the elbow against the rib in counterpoint to the rhythm.

Antelope (eland) dance.

A Gentle People in the Thirstland

Art

More than 6,000 sites of Bushmen rock art are scattered throughout southern Africa. The paintings and etchings describe—in shades of beige, ochre, blood red, brown, yellow, and white—the hunt, the animals hunted, the collection of honey, the gathering of vegetables, and camp life. The shapes of the figures—craggy and sticklike—reflect the distorted vegetation in the harsh environment in which the Bushmen live.

Rock art was part of the ancient culture. A little more than 100 years ago, many Bushmen identified the paintings as theirs. Today, few Bushmen associate the paintings with their people. According to Laurens van der Post, it is believed that the last painter was killed in the Basuto Hills in a raid by the trekkers late in the nineteenth century. As he fell, the different colors of paint that were stored in 10 little horns attached to a zebra thong tied round his waist tumbled into a design upon the ground.

This story of the last painter is not entirely true, for a few years ago there was an exhibit of modern Bushmen art at the Louvre and several other museums around the world. At the Bushmen settlement in Phuduhudu, several artists—Kua, Zhoa, and Sho—still illustrate the stories of their people. Poetry, music, and art are matters of survival for these Bushmen. They sense that if art should die, their civilization would cease as well.

Customs

In the story "Bow and Arrow," puberty rites of Bushmen boys are briefly mentioned. In each Bushman's life, a rite of passage must be undergone to allow full membership into the group.

For the boys, a ceremony is performed after reaching puberty and showing proficiency in hunting. The men and several magicians take the boys away for one month. At first the boys are half starved; they have no fire and no meat—just berries, roots, and a little water.

During this period, many sacred dances are performed day and night. The boys cannot speak to young unmarried women. Some tribes even perform a kind of tattooing. Several cuts are made between the eyebrows or on their backs between their shoulder blades. After this operation, the boys are regarded as men and may marry and participate in the council with men.

For a girl, the attainment of puberty is marked by the first menses. She is set aside in a tiny hut. When she leaves the hut, her eyes must be focused on the ground. She must not venture far. The girl is not allowed to eat game killed by the young men, only game killed by her father. There are many legends about men who look at girls during this time. These men, according to the stories, have been turned to stone, stars, or talking trees. Girls who disobey turn into frogs or are carried off by a bull to their death. In the story "The Rain Bull," Tishay is abducted by the Rain Bull in an adaptation of this myth.

In the !Kung tribe, the women and two men dressed with the horns of an eland perform a dance in a pubescent girl's honor. The *motif* of this dance is the courtship of the eland bull.

With rituals and customs, the Bushman tries hard to guard against "loss of soul." This is demonstrated in the story "All the Stars and the Heavens." In this story, the Bushmen are not worried about the betrayal of Mohombu and Radiance. Rather, the Bushmen care more that Mohombu could not feel, that he was not connected to the magical spirit inside himself. Bushmen feel they cannot exist without their souls; without the stars and the heavens they would surely die, would surely vanish.

Death and Burial

> *The day we die a soft breeze*
> *will wipe out our footprints*
> *in the sand. When the wind*
> *dies down, who will tell the*
> *timelessness that once we*
> *walked this way in the dawn*
> *of time?*
>
> —Bushman song

The origin of death is recorded in "The Hare's Split Lip," a story about the Moon and the Hare. Little is known about how the Bushmen interpret the causes of death. In some instances the cause of death is considered accidental—a poison arrow, the bite of a lion, or starvation. The Bushmen are not always satisfied with natural causes but suspect a sorcerer or supernatural power to have caused death.

If Bushmen die under normal circumstances, they are buried with all their possessions not far from their *scherm*, or hut. The body is arranged with knees drawn up against the breast in a sleeping position. The knees are pointed in the direction of the east to prepare the Bushman for the next journey.

Burial can be refused if the person did not die a good death. Sometimes burial is impossible, especially for the elderly, who are actually abandoned in times of drought. Many think this practice is inhumane, but when one considers that the life of the whole group depends on rapid movement toward food and water, it is understandable. If water is found, the Bushmen immediately send a runner back to assist the abandoned party. Others remain to set up camp.

On the day of his or her death, the Bushman knows the spirit will join the wind in making clouds for rain to fall upon the land. It is said that even the stars know; one will fall with the announcement of the death. It is also said that a *hamerkop*, or lightning bird, will fly over the camp, calling out to announce the death.

Religion and Magic

Take from this child, the
heart of a child and give
him the heart of a star.

—a mother's prayer for her son

The Bushmen believe the stars are the great hunters of old. The fable "All the Stars and the Heavens" demonstrates the amazing mystery that the stars are people who can come to Earth to live. The Bushmen believe it is possible to transform themselves into an animal any time they please.

Even the wind is alive to the Bushmen; it is like a giant child. If the child lies down, it blows. If the child kicks, leaves and sand fly about. What would happen if this wind-child had no father to build a protective shelter and to discipline him? What would happen if this wind-child did not have a mother as well? Would the world itself blow away?

Most primitive societies tell *cosmogonic myths*, myths that tell the origin of the universe. The Bushmen's creation story comes from a mystical moment in time. Their creation goddess, Tumtumbolosa, is pregnant with the whole world. In the tale "How the World Came into Being," Tumtumbolosa explodes, and out tumbles all of creation.

In "Mantis Comes to Life," we find the birth of the Bushman god, the Praying Mantis. Mantis holds a special place in the Bushman's heart, for Bushmen believe great things come from small beginnings, just as the mantis comes into being from a tiny egg. The Bushman's pointed face and slanted eyes are like the face and eyes of the mantis.

Though the Mantis is their god, the Bushmen do not worship it; they pray only to the moon and the stars.

One of the most magical characteristics of the Bushmen is their deep connection with their god. At certain times, a male Bushman claims he feels a "tapping within himself." At once, he will stop and sit alone to listen, to figure out which way this "tapping" is telling him to go. It appears this physical sensation tells him of things to come, much like a sixth sense or a gift of intuition.

For the Bushmen, religion plays a part in all life: from the hunt to the dance in honor of the feast; from rituals to art; from the telling of stories to the pounding heart.

Folklore and Myths

The story is like the wind.
It comes from a far-off
place and we feel it.

—Xhabbo, a Bushman character in *A Story Like the Wind*

Bushman myths depict a prehistoric world seen through the eyes of a childlike people. Storytelling has long been a source of great joy to the Bushmen. In the heat of the day or surrounding the fire by night, they recount various fables of the "old race," when people were animals; tales of the great hunt; and adventures of their god who, taking the form of a praying mantis, plays tricks on other animals. The Bushmen's laughter is contagious. At the end of a funny story, they throw back their heads and roar with pleasure.

Favorite Animals

The ostrich, who appears in many stories, is considered by the Bushmen to be the greatest bird in all of Africa. The Bushman Kataye, in the tale "Why Ostriches Don't Fly," is like the titan Prometheus of Greek myth, who steals fire from heaven for all of mankind. The loss of fire causes the ostrich to never lift her wing again; forever after she is so afraid of losing her head that she sets an egg outside her nest as a reminder of her duty to sit on the egg. In "The Brave Mrs. Ostrich," we see how courageous she can be as she protects her young.

No Bushman would ever dare shoot an ostrich or her family during its protective dance of courage, although they do enjoy eating ostrich meat and eggs. The egg alone is a great treasure. It is used as a canteen to carry water. The Bushmen etch designs on it or chisel beads from the shell.

Honey, like water, is very precious to the Bushman. Honey is a treat, a golden prize. There are two creatures in the desert who share this love of honey: the honey-guide, a bird, and the honey-badger, a ratel. "In Search of the Golden Prize" is a tale about the honey-guide and the ratel leading Katuc on an adventure to find honey. The honey-bird is known throughout Africa as the most magical bird of all. The bravest of all animals is the ratel. Its skin is so thick that neither the sting of the bee nor the fangs of a mamba can penetrate it. The honey-badger will even enter snakes' holes and fight with them there, all odds against it.

The Bushmen say that once the ratel had a fight with a lion. The lion killed the ratel. But the lion was so mangled by the ratel he couldn't lie down to eat it. Since then, even the lion avoids the ratel. Despite its fierceness, the ratel shares its honey with the honey-guide.

The most revered creature of all is the eland. Thousands of paintings have been made of this antelope. It is said that he carried the Bushman god, the walking stick Mantis, between his toes as the clicking of his leathered hooves echoed over the desert. Another antelope, the gemsbok, plays as great a role in the myths of the Bushmen as the eland. In the story "Gemsbok Gets His Horns," the gemsbok is a miserable creature until he steals the horns of the ostrich and thereby steals some of her color.

The Life of the Bushmen Today

*Life on earth is that part of the soul's journey
toward eternity.*

—Kora Kora Due
the "White Bushman" of Phuduhudu

Time is running out for the Kalahari Bushmen. For more than 10,000 years they have lived on land that others consider to be harsh and hostile. Yet they have remained attuned to their environment, in balance with nature, never taking more than what they need to survive. Now, with Western civilization encroaching upon their society, as well as 15 years of drought, it seems their unique lifestyle may die.

It is estimated that there are more than 60,000 Bushmen scattered throughout Angola, parts of South Africa, Namibia, and Botswana. Most have been moved into cities or moved close to a *borehole* for water. In early 1995, Laurens van der Post noted there were only 13 true Bushmen left, living as nomads and subsiding off the land as hunter–gatherers. But in late August 1995, deep in the Kalahari at Molapo, my group discovered there were no nomads to be found. Instead, we found two tribes, the Gikwe and the Gxannakwe, greatly dependent on the Botswanan government for their monthly supply of water. These two tribes live alongside the Bakgalagadi, "the people of the place that dried up long ago." The Bakgalagadi farm and raise goats and cattle. In these lean times, they employ the Bushmen and pay them with food.

Children.

A Gentle People in the Thirstland

The Bushmen are no longer wrapped lightly in loincloths, but are covered with Western clothing, even UCLA sweatshirts and New York Yankee baseball caps. It is rumored there have been many complaints by the Botswanan people about Bushmen being photographed nude.

More than 20 tribes live in Botswana. The ruling tribes are the Bamangwato, Bakwena, and Bawangketse. The Basarwa, or Bushmen, are ranked as the lowest tribe of all. For this reason, a war goes on for their hearts and minds. Many inhabitants of Botswana want to leave the Bushmen as they are, as hunter–gatherers. Others fight to assimilate them into the dominant society.

Many are tired of supporting the Bushmen with monthly deliveries of water. Some have proposed all Bushmen be moved to live in cities. The Bushmen say, "If you move us, you must move our land, you must move our animals we hunt, our melons, our plants. How else will we live?" Some bands of Bushmen have moved to the towns and cities and are struggling to make ends meet. A few families have moved to ranches to work.

Whether or not the Bushmen of Molapo are moved, their society is rapidly crumbling. The children are bused to school for long periods of time. No longer are they taught to hunt, to gather food from the veld. No longer are they told stories, and the dancing light in their eyes dies.

The filmmaker John Marshall has followed the Ju/'hoansi Bushmen in Nyae Nyae, Namibia, for more than 30 years. Since 1989, this tribe of Bushmen on the Gautcha Pan have been trying to destroy the lie that Bushmen are only hunter–gatherers. The Ju/'hoansi are striving hard against dry boreholes and encroaching ranchers to develop farms. Even the lions, which the law says they cannot kill, pose a threat to the raising of cattle.

It is difficult even for those of us living in the highly industrialized West to keep up with our rapidly changing world. Think of the changes in our world within the last 100 years: airplanes, electricity, telephones, television, flights to the moon, nuclear power, satellites. Computer technology, cyberspace, and genetic research have transformed the world yet again in only the last 15 years.

It is difficult to imagine a river wide enough to fill the gap between our complicated Western way of life and the hunter–gatherer society of Bushmen, who have been wandering the Kalahari Desert for 10,000–40,000 years. Bringing them into the modern world is even more difficult. Yet for the Bushmen to sustain their traditional way of life is nearly impossible.

Given this impossibility, I have taken their stories and retold them in our language. If their society should be overwhelmed by contemporary forces, their stories will not. They will live on in our hearts and minds, offering us a connection to the soul of the earth, to the soul of the stars, to ourselves, and to our god. In this way we will remember a people—the Kalahari Bushmen—who lived this connection every day.

A Gentle People in the Thirstland

A trap is set to catch a duiker, small antelope.

Kua draws an ostrich.

Ostrich-egg canteens.

Rasekamo stands proud in typical Bushman attire.

Disjointed dead trees influence Bushman art.

Tracks of an animal in the sand.

A modern scherm.

A modern woman.

Ra di Tshipi, "Man of Iron." (*Photograph by Janet P. Lewis.*)

A group of Bushmen at Molapo.

Bayeti serves mealie meal.

Mother with her three children.

Grandfather and granddaughter at Molapo.
(Photograph by Janet P. Lewis.)

All the Stars and the Heavens

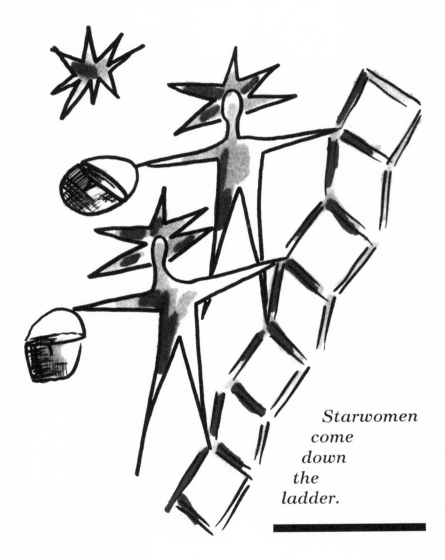

Starwomen
come
down
the
ladder.

The Bushmen tell a story
about a man
in the early days of the race
*   who captured a herd of cattle.*

Outside Mohombu's scherm
the Morning Star twinkled lively
*   above the Maluti Mountains.*

Mohombu wiped the sleep from his eyes
and caught sight of something rare:
*   A ladder tumbled down from the heavens.*

A bit surprised,
he rubbed his eyes once more,
*   and still the vision remained.*

All of a sudden,
the most delicate creatures
he had ever seen
climbed down
the ladder,
step by step.
Like fire,
*   light radiated from their bodies.*

Mohombu said to himself,
"Why, these young women are
*   from the people of the stars."*

All the Stars and the Heavens

When the starwomen touched the earth,
they began to dance and sing
        and then disappeared over the horizon.

Mohombu quickly wrapped
his hartebeest cloak around him
        and followed close behind.

Their soothing sound swept him along until
        it carried him to his cattle's thorny shelter.

Hiding quietly in the bushes,
he watched the starwomen milk
his very own
        black-and-white stippled cattle.

Enraged,
Mohombu flew out of hiding,
cursing and shouting and chasing
        after them.

The starwomen scattered,
dancing, singing,
as quickly as
they could
        until they reached the ladder.

As they climbed
high,
out of his reach,
he caught the leg of
        the prettiest star.

Mohombu swept her up into his arms
and carried her home.
He called her "Radiance"
        and asked for her hand in marriage.

She graciously responded,
"Yes,
but only if
        you promise never to open my basket."

"Ah!
That is not too much to ask,"
        Mohombu replied.

Mohombu and Radiance married
and began their new life.
Radiance gathered firewood, collected veldkos,
and cooked for Mohombu
while he hunted
        and looked after his spotted cows.

One day, all this changed.
While Radiance was away, busy with her gathering,
Mohombu hovered over her basket
        until curiosity got the best of him.

When Radiance returned home,
she looked into his eyes—
and knew.
The smile disappeared from her face,
and she cried,
"Ahh!
        You opened it."

"And why not?" he said,
and then began shouting,
"Cannot a husband know
        what's going on in his own house?"

"And you found nothing?"
        she questioned.

"Of course not,
silly woman!"
        Mohombu replied.

"You mean,
you couldn't see
all the wonderful things
I had brought
from the stars and the heavens
for us both?"
        she questioned once more.

"No."
        He sighed with deep regret.

Radiance was sad.
She turned her back on him
and slowly vanished into the sunset.
        And was never seen on the earth again. ℘

This tale is derived from a story Laurens van der Post heard when he was a
child. It was told to him by his Bushman nanny.

All the Stars and the Heavens

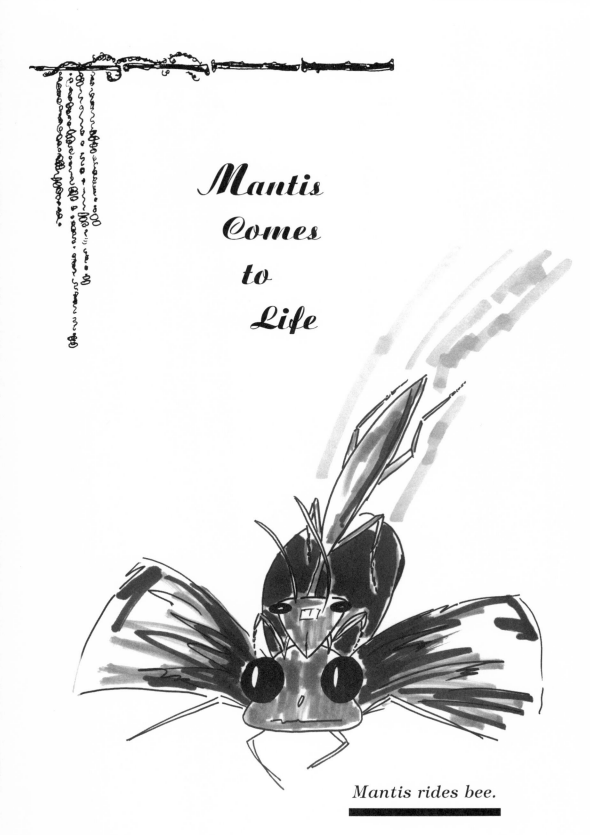

Mantis Comes to Life

Mantis rides bee.

Long before
there were people
in the world,
   Mantis was.

Dark, windy waters
covered the entire earth.
So Mantis had only
one way to travel:
Bee.
Bee,
the honey-maker,
the ultimate image of wisdom,
carried Mantis
over this watered world.
The praying mantis,
though small
and shaped much like a twig,
was becoming a heavy,
   heavy burden for Bee.

"Oh! Mantis,
oh, Mantis,
can I not go down
to find you a place to perch?"
   Bee questioned his guide and burden.

Good Mantis
searched with his big beady eyes.
He searched and he searched
   and he searched.

Mantis Comes to Life

But there was just no earth.
He cried,
"Oh! Dear Bee,
can you not see
the planet is just
    a murk!"

The Bee flew slower,
and the slower he flew,
the bigger became his burden.
The bigger his burden,
the lower he flew,
    the nearer became the water.

And then,
at last,
upon the water
a great white lily floated.
Half-opened and
awaiting the sun to rise,
the lily accepted
    Bee's load.

"Oh! Mantis, here,
at last we find
a place to rest,
a place to lie,"
the Bee exclaimed as he collapsed
and took his final breath,
    and died.

Now,
warm and safe
from all the wind,
the Mantis lay
   inside this flower.

And in the early morning sun,
Mantis came alive again.
And there the first Bushman
was born.
Born on the Lily.
   Born in the Sun. ♨

I originally read this tale in Elizabeth S. Helfman's *The Bushmen and Their Stories* (1971).

How the World Came into Being

*Tumtumbolosa
pregnant with the
whole world.*

Long ago,
when the planet
was not yet
full of people,
and no one had even
dreamed of animals
or plants,
there lived the
goddess of the Gikwe
named Tumtumbolosa.
At that time,
only a few little Gikwe
     walked the earth.

Then,
Tumtumbolosa died.
And as she did,
her stomach grew and grew.
It appeared that
Tumtumbolosa was bloated.
Her stomach continued
to grow and grow,
becoming bigger and bigger
and more and more
like a giant balloon,
until
BOOM!
Tumtumbolosa exploded.
And out burst
all the stars,

which flew into the sky,
the moon,
the sun.
A river overflowed,
raging in white turbulence.
As it moved along the earth,
    a forest grew.

Tumtumbolosa's
stomach
caused much commotion on the earth,
for all of a sudden
out tumbled
every living creature
from A to Z:
antelopes of many kinds—steenbok,
    springbok, duiker, kudu;
water buffalo;
and all kinds of cats—cheetahs, bobcats, leopards;
barking dogs;
and elephants;
frogs that croaked ever so loudly;
towering giraffes as tall as the trees in the forest;
hippopotami;
ibis;
jackals;
beautiful black-and-white birds, the Korhaans;
lazy lions;
mamba snakes;
newts, salamanders;
ostriches;
crowned plovers;
quaggas, mountain zebras;

rhinosaurus;
stinging scorpions;
tortoises;
umbrella trees;
lappet-faced vultures;
wildebeests;
Xhosa, a tribe of Bantu;
yellow mongooses;
hartman zebras.
The whole lot of them
    filled the forest.

In the daytime,
the little Gikwe
were burnt by the sun,
so they ran for shade in the forest.
Late that evening,
looking up through the trees,
they saw the sky
and, for the first time,
    thousands of stars shining brightly.

And just think,
it all flowed from
the pregnant stomach
of the Great Creator,
    Tumtumbolosa.

Derived from a tale told by Izak Barnard under the stars of an African night.

A child with mother and others looking on.

The Hare's Split Lip

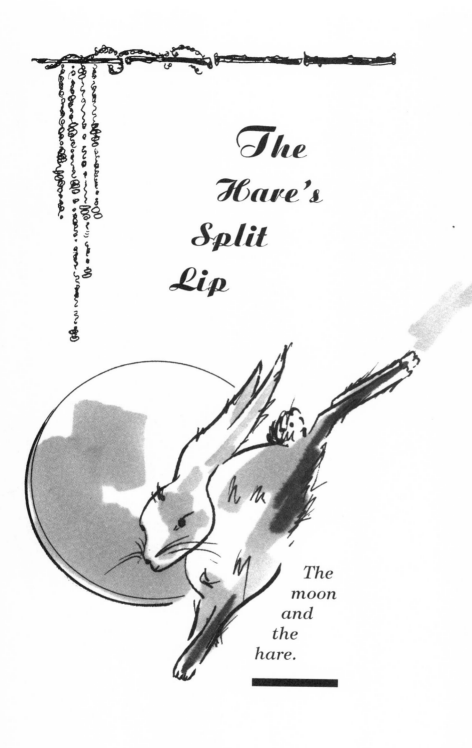

The moon and the hare.

℘ A long time ago,
the moon
saw that the people on earth
were frightened
of death.
"This should not be,"
she said to herself,
        "I must reassure them."

So the moon called out
to one of the
fastest animals,
the hare,
and told him,
"Run and tell
the people on earth
not to be afraid.
For don't they see
that each month I die
only to rise again?
So too they will
        rise as well."

The hare
ran off in such a hurry
that the faster he went,
the more twisted the message became.
The hare declared
to all the people,
"The moon says

The Hare's Split Lip

that unlike the moon
who in dying
is brought back to life again,
*   you will die and not return."*

The moon caught wind
of this twisted tale
and in all her fury declared,
"I must put a stop to this,
*   for this is how rumors begin!"*

So the moon
punished the rabbit—
*   she hit him on the lip.*

To this day,
the Bushmen believe that because
the hare twisted the moon's message,
the lip of the hare is split,
he has no home,
he sleeps out in the open,
suffering from the heat of the sun,
the storms,
*   and the wind that blows.* ✂

Derived from a tale in Dr. Willem H. I. Bleek's *Reynard the Fox in South Africa* (1864). Dr. Bleek was the first to study the language and record the stories of several Bushman prisoners. The oldest prisoner, Xhabbo (whose name is the Bushman word for dream) was the most prolific of storytellers.

The Hare's Split Lip

The
Rain
Bull

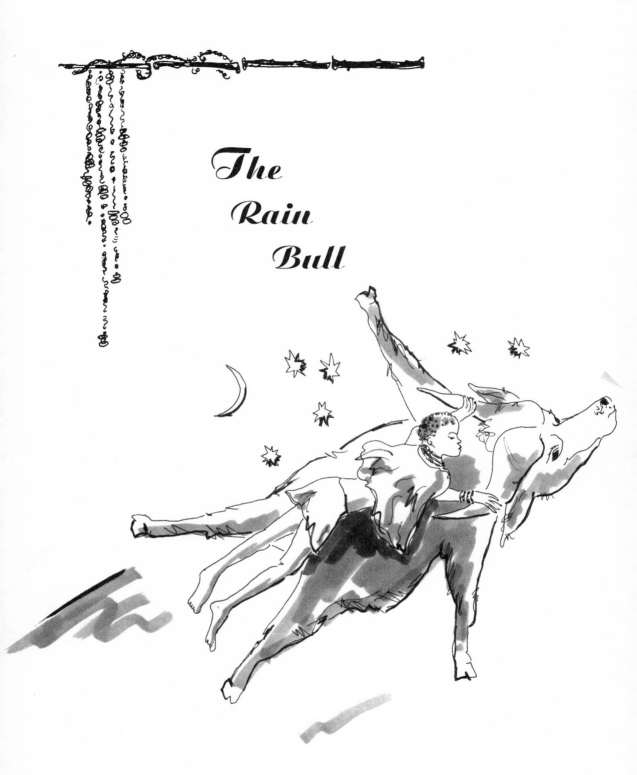

The rain bull.

A long time ago,
at the beginning of time,
Rain,
in the form of a bull,
    came to earth.

Trotting through the mist,
Rain smelled a fragrance
and followed the scent
until he found
a young woman
    named Tishay.

Tishay exclaimed,
"Oh! You are very beautiful!
    From whence did you come?"

"I am Rain!
I come from above
to shower the earth
and make plenty,"
    he claimed.

Tishay obviously
liked Rain,
for upon his head
she scattered
    the most fragrant of herbs.

He asked Tishay,
"Please come and ride with me.

Come see the world.
Please, oh, please.
        You simply must come and see!"

So she climbed upon his back,
and together they trotted
and trotted across the sky.
They passed the stars,
they passed the moon,
the lakes, the trees,
the earth,
until Tishay grew very tired
and cried,
"Oh! Mr. Rain
can we not stop?
        I fear I've grown to ache."

Gently,
Rain set her down
beside a tree,
along a bubbling brook.
In deep reverence
she massaged his hide
with fragrant herbs,
        and he fell fast asleep.

That night,
Tishay slipped away
        and walked the long road home.

As she silently moved across the land,
she rubbed and rubbed and scrubbed
the scent of the bull away.
And what remained

was the sweetest smell,
the smell of the gentle rain.

In the morning,
Rain awakened.
Still with the thought
that Tishay was there,
he trotted off to the stream,
to the source of the bubbling spring.
As he bent his head
for a long cool drink,
he saw his dear reflection.
Tishay was not to be found.
    But it did not really matter.

At last, he knew where he belonged—
here, with the water,
here, with the source.
Here he could make life-giving rain
for all the people upon the earth.
And now more than ever,
he could do it far better
for a woman named Tishay,
and the sweetest smell of herbs
    would be with him forever.

Derived from "The Rain Bull and the Girl" in Arthur Markowitz's *The Rebirth of the Ostrich* (1971). Markowitz came under the spell of the Bushman lore when he met a retired German missionary. This missionary ministered to the Bushmen for many years, and though they never grasped his faith, he followed them, studied their culture and accumulated their tales. This tale was also published as "Rain and the Young Woman" in Elizabeth S. Helfman's *The Bushmen and Their Stories* (1971).

The
First
Tug-of-War

The tug-of-war.

Ra di Tshipi,
stands as strong
and as true
as the meaning of his name,
        "Man of Iron."

He tells a story
        of the early days.

In those days,
the Bushmen
and the Non-Bushmen
were one nation.
But then,
God came to earth
and gave them a rope made
        of grass fiber and reim.

God declared,
"All the people must
        take this rope and tug on it."

And so,
the first great tug-of-war
        came into being.

The First Tug-of-War

The people pulled
and tugged,
pulled and tugged.
No one fell down.
No one gave up.
     Pulled and tugged.

Pulled and tugged
until they
pulled and tugged
so hard
that the rope
split in two,
and all the men
and women
     fell to the ground.

The Bushmen landed hard.
They looked down into their hands
only to find they had
pulled away the grass fiber.
The Non-Bushmen
sat smiling,
for they had
pulled and tugged
until the strong leather
     remained in their hands.

From then on,
the Non-Bushmen had cattle and reims,
     but the Bushmen had only the things of the veld.

Ra di Tshipi said,
"If there should ever be
another tug-of-war,
I will warn the Bushman.
I will tell him
to pull and tug,
to pull and tug
so very hard
until he has won
        the leather half."

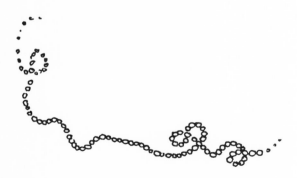

A similar tale is found in Arthur Markowitz's *The Rebirth of the Ostrich* (1971).

Bow
and
Arrow

Kora Kora Due shoots Kesedilwe with arrow.

Kesedilwe leaped in the air!

Kora Kora Due waited.
He hoped
her response was
out of sheer happiness.
But,
it was most likely
from the shock,
for she swatted
at it
      as though a fly.

Kora Kora Due's heart pounded,
for he feared
      she'd snap it in two.

Instead,
Kesedilwe pulled
the arrow from her rump,
observing
the
careful detail
of its
craftmanship.
She turned
toward the direction
of the shot,
caught Kora Kora Due's eye,
and grinned
      with all her might.

Bow and Arrow

In return,
Kora Kora Due smiled
and sighed
with great relief.
Then, stretching his arms
out straight,
he clenched his fist
and began
a tribal dance
of love,
of marriage,
for the woman
of his choice
had not
destroyed love's design.
Kora Kora Due knew in his heart,
     Kesedilwe would soon be his wife.

With his newfound happiness,
Kora Kora Due began
to wander about
the bush
somewhat aimlessly:
a tell-tale sign
     that this Bushman was in love.

Yet, to be dreamy
is quite unusual
for a nomad Bushman,
because survival in the Kalahari Desert
is of the utmost importance.
He must be practical, resourceful.

In three days,
scorched by a 120-degree sun,
with no water in sight,
a man can lose his life,
        taking others along with him.

However,
Kora Kora Due continued a walkabout
with visions of
the first time
he laid eyes on Kesedilwe,
the first time
        they danced together.

Kora Kora Due remembered that,
during puberty,
he went through
the rigors of an initiation,
the rites of passage
from a boy to a man,
for an entire month.
He studied the tribal lore
of his people.
He learned the customs
from the men of his tribe.
He proved himself to be
a good provider,
by making an excellent bow and arrow
and showing his skill
        in stalking and killing game.

Although
the young boys
were restricted
from all conversation
with young women,
their eyes were free to roam.
Kora Kora Due asked the others about Kesedilwe
and learned that
she was an orphan
in his cousin's tribe.
It took all the strength
he could muster
to stay away.
He didn't speak out.
       He didn't break the rule.

But watch her he did.

He loved the way Kesedilwe moved when
she danced with the other women in the camp.
There was an innocence, a freshness.
He could see she was creative,
for she had elegantly woven tiny ostrich egg beads
into a band around her head.
A handpainted ostrich egg
was tied around her waist,
full of the Bushman's most precious resource,
       water.

Every day
he woke up thinking of her,
hoping to catch a glimpse
       once again.

During the last night of the initiation,
Kora Kora Due played a melodious instrument,
a simple mouth bow,
before all the !Kung Bushmen.
He had carved it
from a bamboo reed.
It made a hollow, whistling sound,
like the howling wind
in the trees.
He hoped she'd like it.
*   Hoped she'd dance to it.*

She did.

His heart pounded
faster than the beat of the drums,
as he joined her
in the dance around the fire
with the others.
A lump formed in his throat.
Not a word came out.
But it did not seem to matter,
for the evening sped
as fast as it was
pleasurable.
In their togetherness,
they laughed,
celebrated his new birth,
stirred up the dust a bit,
and ate
*   of the big game from the hunt.*

And so
the daily visits began
to his cousin's tribe.
Sometimes
Kora Kora Due would arrive
at Kesedilwe's scherm
early in the morning
to light her fire.
Once he brought her the most
treasured nuts of the bush,
the Mangetti, much like an almond.
She knew it had taken him
weeks to collect them.
She cracked one,
and gave him half as
she ate the other.
Kora Kora Due knew that
this was a sign of her great interest,
and he began his preparation
    for the proposal.

He rushed off immediately
to begin the hunt.
All day
he searched
for the perfect
gemsbok.
When he found her
he shot her with a poisoned arrow
and chased her
across ten miles of desert,
    until the gemsbok collapsed.

He then
carried her home.
Over the course of a week,
he carefully prepared the hide
for a coat,
        for his bride.

And lastly,
Kora Kora Due carved
a tiny three-inch bow,
like cupid's own,
from a sliver of the gemsbok's bone.
With the utmost care,
he made
tiny arrows
to match the bow,
out of stems
of sturdy grass
that grew near the water.
He stained the tips
with a special love potion
and placed these in
a tiny quiver
formed from the quill
        of a Kori bustard.

One morning,
Kora Kora Due
decided to stalk the woman of his choice.
He hid
quietly
in the bush.

He waited for Kesedilwe to
join the other !Kung women
in doing their chores.
Daily,
the women
searched the veld
to collect
roots, bulbs,
ground nuts,
berries, melons,
leguaan, tortoises,
locusts, flying ants,
birds and birds' nests,
*   and wood.*

When Kesedilwe came near,
*   Kora Kora Due shot her with the arrow.*

We all know her response,
*   and his.*

And so,
early the next morning,
Kora Kora Due arrived at his
cousin's camp.
He found Kesedilwe
sitting before the fire
with her adopted grandmother.
Kora Kora Due placed
the beautiful gemsbok coat
around her.

Kesedilwe smiled
and, with a delightful giggle,
wrapped her arms around herself
    to feel the warmth of her wedding gift.

And to all the Bushmen,
    the marriage was now secured.

Laurens van der Post demonstrates that the Bushman male shoots an arrow to make his claim on a future mate in his film *The Rain Song*, part of the series entitled The Lost World of the Kalahari.

Woman shaves Raphionachmal burkei, *a tuber much like a potato. If there is no water to drink, she will squeeze the shavings for liquid. When water is plentiful, the shavings are used to wash.*

Where Are All the Big Feet?

Pishiboro's elephant wife with lovely beads.

Late one night,
Pishiboro, a god of the Bushmen,
and his younger brother
were deeply sleeping.
Pishiboro's elephant wife
took the two brothers
and rolled them between her thighs
and squashed them.
Pishiboro's brother said,
"Quick! While it is still dark,
let us run away from this evil wife of yours
        before she kills us!"

All night they walked
and they walked,
until they had left "the place that is all dried up,"
until they had disappeared deep into the
        Mopane Forest.

The next day,
when they thought
they had travelled far enough away,
Pishiboro's brother saw the elephant
chasing after them.
He shouted,
"Quick! Quick!
Run and hide.
        I shall handle this."

Where Are All the Big Feet?
49

So,
Pishiboro
ran away
and climbed up high
in a giant Mopane tree.
When the elephant wife arrived,
the young brother replied,
"Hello! I see you have a great big tick in your flesh.
    Let me take it out for you."

The elephant wife smiled and said,
    "Would you, please?"

"Indeed!"
the brother agreed.
Then, he took a camel-thorn
    and pricked her chest below her lovely beads.

"Ow! You're hurting me!"
    she screamed.

"Oh! Yes, of course—
the tick has buried itself quite deeply.
Let me try again, once more."
And so Pishiboro's brother tried again.
He pierced her heart,
    and she died.

The young brother
built a roaring fire
to roast the breast of his brother's wife.
Then, he seated himself atop her body,
    eating the fine elephant.

It just so happened that Pishiboro
was hiding downwind from this glorious smell.
And, of course,
    he came running.

But when he realized what his brother had done,
Pishiboro cried in anger,
"How can this be,
that my very brother kills my wife
    and, now, sits so proudly upon her?"

His brother nonchalantly handed Pishiboro
a piece of roasted elephant
and scornfully declared,
"Oh! You bloody fool,
laziest of men.
You thought her your wife,
    yet you married meat instead."

Pishiboro agreed,
"It is true."
Then he seated himself before the fire
    for one big feast.

But Pishiboro's brother was so hungry
he rushed forward to cut more meat,
and pierced the elephant's vein instead.
Oh, did her blood flow!
So fast that they tried to dig a hole to stop it.
So fast that they tried to fill their mouths to drink it.
So fast that it rushed all the way to the Kalahari,
    to the foot of her family's scherm.

Where Are All the Big Feet?

Once more,
Pishiboro shouted at his brother,
"Oh, you fool!
It was enough to have my wife wanting us dead.
Now, the whole Big Feet herd will stampede
        us red!"

So angry were the elephants
that they came marching out of the
        Kalahari desert.

In the distance,
they heard the elephants stomp.
In the distance
they heard the elephants chomp—
their most favorite food of all,
        the Mopane leaf.

Pishiboro's brother giggled,
"Look! Look how funny the elephants walk!"
For it is true
that, unlike other mammals,
the elephant is so terribly heavy,
he lifts one foot at a time,
        which makes for the oddest of lopes.

"SHHH!"
Pishiboro whispered.
"If you say their name,
if you laugh at Big Feet,
you'll make them horribly bitter.
        Then we most surely shall die!"

The elephants began to chase Pishiboro's brother.
The brother cried,
    "Help! Pishiboro, help!"

Immediately,
Pishiboro leaped onto the back of an elephant
and passed wind.
The elephant died.
Then he jumped on the elephants
one by one.
He tooted
and he tooted.
The elephants died
one by one,
until there was just one—
Old Foot.
The largest elephant,
with the longest tusks,
had reached,
had hooked
    Pishiboro's brother.

Pishiboro climbed high in the tallest of Mopanes.
He dropped down on the largest of elephants,
on top of Old Foot.
And he tooted,
and he tooted.
Then, he tooted big, this time.
The elephant bull dropped dead
    with a BOOM!

Thus,
Pishiboro
had killed all the elephants
of the Kalahari.
That is why
there is not a single
elephant
     in the Kalahari today. ✍

Derived from a tale told to Elizabeth Marshall Thomas by the !Kung Bushmen (*The Harmless People*, 1971). Pishiboro is another name for their god, the praying mantis. Pishiboro appears in two forms: a mantis or a man.

Where Are All the Big Feet?

In
Search
of the
Golden Prize

The bird, the ratel, and the boy.

One day,
as Katuc
was wandering
through the bush,
he heard
the cry
of the
honey-diviner
ringing out
　　　　loud, clear.

She fluttered
about
high in the
Camelthorn tree,
singing,
　　　　"Quick! Quick! Honey . . . quick!"

A smile of delight
spread across
Katuc's face,
and with deep reverence
he replied,
"Oh!
You,
the most magical bird
of the desert,
you,
the leader of the wise.

Yes,
I hear you
and
I am coming
      as quickly as you are flying."

Katuc's
pace quickened,
and with baited breath
he followed the
gilded bird
down the path
      toward the golden prize.

Another cry,
a strange whistle,
      echoed over the desert.

Katuc stopped short
to listen
attentively.
He longed
for the sound
to end in laughter,
laughter
      of a deep kind.

It did.

"Look! Look! Look!
Oh! Person with wings, Look!
Here I come!"
      cried the ratel.

Katuc grinned
and cackled back his reply:
"Oh!
You,
the honey-badger,
bravest of the brave,
what gives us the
privilege of your presence
this fine warm day?
Will you join us
for this rare
        adventure, as well?"

The badger
immediately
fell in line
between the bird
and the boy
and on the hunt went.
What lay before
them,
Katuc could only hope.
Yet,
he tramped on,
marvelling
at the two.
They blazed a trail
before him,
with the bird's
light cheery song
and the badger's whistling response,
and his spoor
        detailed in the sand.

The adventure made him recall the first meeting he had with this ancient bird. He was just four years old. The honey-guide appeared before Katuc and his father and led them on a trek through the desert that lasted all day.

At dusk, they came upon the bee's nest. It was empty. In response, the bird screamed out her sad song and then, a long silence. Out of sheer exhaustion, young Katuc sat down and tears rolled down his face. But his father immediately began singing praises to their guide.

On the way home that night, Katuc's father wrapped his arm around his son and shared a very important secret: "One must always follow the honey-bird, whether she finds honey or not, for it expresses a kind of friendship to the desert's most magical creature. Otherwise, the guide will forever wonder if we only come to her with greed in our hearts."

> All of a sudden,
> the honey-guide
> lighted upon
> a tree stump
> with a large hole,
> just the right size
> for a beehive.
> And she responded with
>   an elegant and final song.

> Without fear,
> without hesitation,
> the badger
> ran straight at the hive
> and began to dig his way into it.
> In spite of the bees' attack,
> he kept working away.
> He bit the bark and tore it off,
>   until he came to the heart of the honey.

In Search of the Golden Prize

This left Katuc
with the chance to perform
his duty.
First,
in honor of the guide,
he set a handful of
honeycomb
on a branch,
calling out to her with praise,
"O person of wings with the heart of gold,
        take, and eat."

Then,
he placed a cup of
this golden sweetness
on the ground before the
one who made it all possible.
"O braveheart,
hunter of the centipede, the scorpion,
and the great mamba snake,
taste, and see that your reward is great!"
        crooned Katuc.

But
the ratel did not respond.
One cup was not enough
        to match his hunger.

Katuc reached in for another
cup of flowering honey
and laid it down before him.
The ratel,
always determined and fully confident,
        ate with pure delight.

With the last swoop,
Katuc took a handful for himself,
another for his mother,
and left the rest
to the next faithful follower,
  he who trusts the honey-guide.

Laurens van der Post tells a similar story in his children's book, *A Far Off-Place* (1978).

The
Beginning
of
All
Ostriches

The feather.

One day,
a Bushman
named Katuc
from the !O Kung tribe
    killed an ostrich.

The last sign of life,
the remains,
lay
    in front of his hut.

He thought to himself,
Why,
    it's the end of all ostriches.

But in came the wind
and swept a feather
into the air,
tossing and spinning,
as though on wings,
until it landed in a pool of water
    surrounded by reeds and flowers.

The feather
turned about slowly
in the rippling water,
and gradually
it grew
and grew

The Beginning of All Ostriches
65

until
it returned to
        its original state:

A young ostrich.

Once it became strong,
the ostrich began to walk about
        the countryside.

One warm sunny day,
the ostrich poked its beak inside Katuc's
        scherm.

"Well . . . "
Katuc sighed with great relief,
        "It's the beginning of all ostriches." ✆

Originally told by Laurens van der Post in a lecture recorded in *Patterns of Renewal* (1962).

The Beginning of All Ostriches

The
Brave

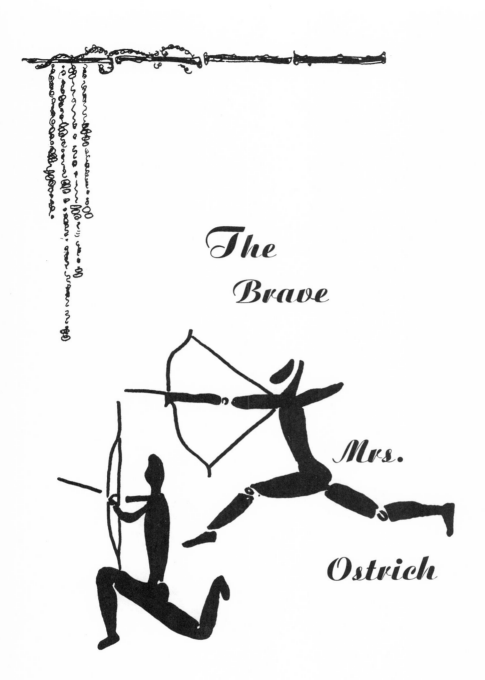

Mrs.

Ostrich

Xhabbo and Mu hunting.

Xhabbo
crouched low
behind the bush.
He set his arrow
on his bow,
took aim
at the great Eland,
pulled back the string,
and—
"Uhg!" Xhabbo groaned
as he fell sideways
        into the sand.

Mu, his hunting companion,
had nudged him
very hard
in the ribs.
"Mu! What's wrong with you?
We could have had
        our favorite meal."

"Psst!"
Mu hissed and pointed
in the other direction.
"Shhhhh!"
For the Ostrich
had caught wind of
their scent.

The Brave Mrs. Ostrich

She immediately
changed her direction
and came running towards them.
The Ostrich
squawked and squealed
        as loud as she could.

Xhabbo
dropped the bow and arrow
and grinned
at Mu.
He whispered,
"Why it's Mrs. Ostrich.
And now she will perform
the dance of the
        courageous!"

Mrs. Ostrich
turned west
and ran away from them,
dragging her left wing
        behind.

Mu turned toward
Xhabbo and laughingly asked,
"I wonder how many
little ostriches
        she's protecting?"

When the Ostrich
noticed that
her supposed pursuers
did not follow,
        she turned back.

The Brave Mrs. Ostrich

Now
she became even more
dramatic,
dragging her wing
      in the sand.

Once more
Mu nudged Xhabbo
      and pointed in the other direction.

There,
running along the ancient pan
of Deception Valley,
was a beautiful proud male ostrich
ushering seventeen ostrichlets.
As quickly as he could,
he pushed them
into the bush
until Mu and Xhabbo
lost sight of them.
They did not
shoot
but sat there in the sand
admiring
      the brave mother.

As soon as
her children were out of sight,
the Ostrich
turned her back
on Mu and Xhabbo
and
ran quickly
      after her children.

The Brave Mrs. Ostrich

Xhabbo and Mu
covered their mouths
      to hide a laugh of pleasure.

For in all of Africa,
there was nothing
more beautiful,
more delightful,
than a brave female ostrich,
with all the skill
of a great actress,
courageously willing
to lose her life,
for the sake of
      her ostrichlets.

In 1956, Laurens van der Post explored the Kalahari Desert in search of the remaining Bushmen. During this adventure, van der Post and his companion, Ben Hatherall, came upon a family of ostriches and saw the mother ostrich carry on a similar drama. The account is recorded in *The Heart of the Hunter* (1961).

The Brave Mrs. Ostrich

Gemsbok Gets His Horns

Ostrich with long, elegant horns.

In the beginning,
all animals were people,
all the pans were plentiful
with water.
Yet, the Gemsbok
was a feeble man,
hornless and grey.
The Ostrich
was colorful
  and had long elegant horns.

The Gemsbok
cried out a challenge
to this elegant and long creature.
"Look,
I bet my four legs
can outrun your
two spindly legs and neck,
which carries far too heavy horns.
Let's have a race and see.
I'll make it even—
  let me carry those horns of yours."

The Ostrich
in all her elongated beauty
smiled and said,
"Well, they are a bit heavy.
Why, that's a grand idea."

Gemsbok Gets His Horns

So she pulled off her horns
and placed them on Gemsbok.
She pulled off some of her color
and painted the face of the Gemsbok.
The Gemsbok
paused before the water
to glance at his reflection
and gloated,
"Now isn't that a sight!"
And indeed it was.
        Even Ostrich agreed.

And so the race began.

The Gemsbok ran fast and far
and chose only
the roughest of stony paths.
The Ostrich's feet
became tender and sore.
She had not a chance,
not one little chance
        to win.

She finally caught sight
of her horns
perched on the head
of the Gemsbok.
He paused quietly,
watching her in her pain.
Ostrich became furious.
She picked up stones.
She hurled them at him.
"Take that!" she said,
as she reached down for more ammunition.
But when she looked up,
        Gemsbok was gone.

Gemsbok Gets His Horns

After a long gallop across the sand,
Ostrich met up with Gemsbok
and tried to recover her horns.
Gemsbok fought back
       with all his might.

Ostrich stepped aside
wisely to gather her thoughts:
"It is quite true that
the horns are much too heavy
for my long legs and neck.
Perhaps, if I give them to him
he shall forever be my friend,
       he shall forever protect me."

And so forever
or as long as the Bushmen
can recall,
Gemsbok and Ostrich
together
roam the plains
in peace,
       in harmony.

Since her childhood, Coral Fourie has traveled in the Kalahari to visit the Bushmen. In her book, *Living Legends of a Dying Culture* (1994), she records this original tale, "How Gemsbok (Oryx) Got His Horns" as told to her by !Abezwa of Mathlo-a-phuduhudu, a woman of the !Xo clan of the Western Kalahari.

Gemsbok Gets His Horns

77

Iponeng walks with her gathering stick and kaross over her shoulder each morning to find food for the day.

The
Race

Ostrich and the turtles.

In the early days,
Ostrich and Tortoise
had an argument.
In his anger,
Tortoise challenged her:
"You continually brag
of your great speed.
Who would win a race between us?
    Let's try and see."

"Oh!
But I am
oh so fast today.
oh so much faster than yesterday,"
    Ostrich replied.

Tortoise
thought to himself,
Well, I'll show Ostrich.
She thinks herself so fast,
but I am ever so clever.
I'll place my tortoise friends
along the path where we're to meet.
We tortoises look alike,
    she'll think they're all me!

Thus,
the race began
between Ostrich and
    the first Tortoise.

The Race

Soon
Ostrich passed the
second Tortoise,
who shouted,
            "My, my
            the farther you go
            the faster I am!"
Ostrich stretched out her neck
            and galloped on her way.

She came upon the
third Tortoise.
He cried,
"My, my
the farther you go
the faster I am!"
Ostrich stretched out
her neck once more
and sprinted
ever so fast
        through the sand.

The further
she ran,
the more exhausted she became,
        and the more the Tortoise
        mocked her.

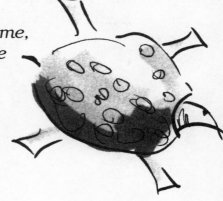

The Race
82

When she reached the last Tortoise,
he exclaimed,
"I've won!
Can't you see?
I've beat you
and I have not one tired
      bone under my shell."

Ostrich,
in great defeat,
in great pain,
collapsed on the ground.
She had run so fast,
so far,
that she had lost all
      the marrow in her bones.

To this day,
the Ostrich has no marrow
in the thigh bones
      of her elegant long legs. ✍

Derived from the story, "Ostrich and Tortoise's Race" in Coral Fourie's *Living Legends of a Dying Culture* (1994). The tale was told to her by N!xau/He, a Bushman from the !Kung of the Tchumkwe area.

The Race

Who Is the Greatest of Them All?

Lion fends off clods of dirt.

In the days of the early race,
an argument rose up between
the Lion and the Ostrich.

"I am the greatest of all,"
boasted the Lion,
"for look at my teeth—
large, white and strong—
and you, like a child,
have not one!"

At that,
the Ostrich replied,
very firmly,
"Ah,
but I am very wise,
for I am many winters old."

"I am much much more
many winters than you!"
the Lion roared.
"Therefore,
let's hear your call,
your call of the wild."

"Arrrrgh! Arrrrrgh!"
she cried.

"ROOOOOAR! ROOOOOAR!"
Lion bellowed,
and his sound echoed
throughout the desert.

Who Is the Greatest of Them All?

Ostrich sat calmly fanning herself,
with a papyrus branch,
from the heat
        of Lion's roar.

"Well,
I see,
you are not frightened
of me,
though you have no teeth
with which to kill,"
        Lion challenged.

"I am tall,
I am great,
great as you.
So, let us go now
and hunt as two,"
        she replied.

On safari,
Lion attacked an eland.
Ostrich attacked the calf.
Lion tore off chunks of meat and chomped.
Ostrich couldn't chew but drank blood
        instead.

The Lion roared once more,
"Hah!
You cannot chew meat without teeth.
        Come here! I'll eat you, too!"

Ostrich ran quickly away
and hid behind the ant-hill.

Lion approached
and circled around the hill.
　　Ostrich moved accordingly.

"Whack! Whack!"
All of a sudden,
Lion was blind.
For Ostrich with her two-toed feet
scratched clods from the hill
　　and threw these at him.

But still he hollered,
"Wait! Wait!
Can't you see?
I am the greatest,
I am he!"

Ostrich continued to throw
ant-hill clods
until the Lion's lights went out.
Then she yelled at the top
of her lungs for all to hear,
"Oh yes,
it is true!
I have no teeth.
But I had a plan—
just look at you.
Now, who would you say
　　is the greatest today?" ✍

Derived from a legend told by the Bushman N!Xau C,umaa at Tchumkwe to
Coral Fourie, author of *Living Legends of a Dying Culture* (1994).

Who Is the Greatest of Them All?

A mother with child strapped to her back wraps the berries of the grewia retinervis, or raisin bush, in her son's shirt. This berry has a nutty flavor and is used to quench one's thirst.

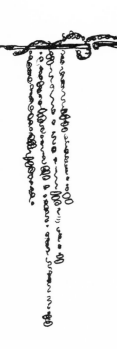

Why Ostriches Don't Fly

*Ostrich warming her toes
and browning her meat.*

*The young Bushman
Kataye
knows why the ostrich
keeps one egg outside
        her nest.*

*It all happened
long ago,
actually,
when Kataye
was walking along
the sandy pathway,
        and he came upon a wonderful smell.*

*Peeking through the branches,
he caught sight of
an ostrich seated next to
a flickering flame.
She was browning her meal.
Kataye wondered,
        How does she make this flame?*

*Early
the next morning,
he sat waiting
        in the bush.*

*The ostrich lifted
her wing,
pulled out fire,
        and proceeded to cook.*

Why Ostriches Don't Fly

Once again
the glorious smell
wafted toward him.
Kataye wanted the fire
      all the more.

I'll take the ostrich
to the most irresistible fruit
of all,
the plum,
high in the Merenda Tree!
      he exclaimed to himself.

And so he did.

The ostrich followed him gladly,
and upon finding the tree,
      she ate heartily.

Kataye said,
"Good, good,
but no,
no, you must
eat higher up.
      It's much better up there."

The ostrich stood on the tips of her
two-toed feet.
As she did,
she raised her wings for balance
      and felt the fire go out of her.

Kataye
had
      stolen it.

The ostrich blinked her
      beady eyes in shock.

She was never quite the same.
Indeed, she became a little strange.
She never flew again.
Perhaps she feared
if she raised her wings
she'd lose what little fire she had left.

And so, forever,
or as long as Kataye has been telling the tale,
the ostrich has kept one egg
outside the nest.
For it was
in a moment of forgetting
that she lost the fire.
Perhaps the egg is a reminder
never to forget,
      never to neglect the life force within her again.

Laurens van der Post told a similar story, which is recorded in *Patterns of Renewal* (1962).

Forever as a reminder, one ostrich egg remains outside the nest.

Glossary

!Kung Bushmen. A subset of Bushmen who live in northwest Botswana or northeast Namibia.

//gwashi. A five-string musical instrument made from the heartwood of a male mangetti tree.

anthropologist. One who studies human beings; a researcher who studies the peoples of the world and their different ways of life.

band. A community of Bushmen hunter–gatherers who travel, hunt, and live together.

Basarwa. Name given to the Bushmen by the Africans.

borehole. A deep well containing semi-permanent water pumped by windmill or engine.

bush. A wild area in Australia or Africa.

Bushmen. A name given to the hunter–gatherer people of southern Africa, the first inhabitants of the Kalahari.

clicks. A sound made by sucking air into the mouth, commonly found in the Bushmen language.

cosmogonic myths. Tales that account for the origin of the universe; stories about creation.

culture. A way of life: music, art, religion, and so on, of a group of people.

drought. A period of time with no rain.

ecosystem. A system made up of a community of animals and plants and their relationship to the physical enviroment.

equilibrium. A state of balance.

game. Wild birds or animals hunted for food.

game reserve. An area preserved for animals in the wild where no hunting is permitted.

hamerkop. Lightning bird.

hunter–gatherers. A group of people who live by hunting game and gathering wild vegetables.

kaross. A leather cape of cured antelope or other kind of skin, worn by Bushmen or used to carry the day's catch.

Khoi-Khoin. The name the Hottentots call themselves.

Khoisan. The racial stock of the Bushmen and the Hottentots. The name derives from Khoi-Khoin, the name the Hottentots call themselves, and San, the name the Hottentots call the Bushmen.

mealie meal. Food recently given to the Bushmen by the government. It has now become a staple of their diet. Mealie meal is a cereal grain similar to grits or cream of wheat.

motif. A main element, idea, or feature.

nomads. A tribe or people with no permanent home.

omuramba. An ancient river bed.

qhwai-xkhwe. A male Bushman.

reim. A strip of leather.

salt pan. An ancient lake (as in Guatscha or Deception Pan).

San. The name the Hottentots call the Bushmen.

scherm. A Bushman hut; a shelter of branches stuck in the ground, bent together, and covered with grass.

setinkane. Thumb piano.

sip wells. A source of water for the Bushmen; one pushes a bamboo stick deep into the sand, then sucks on it to draw water and siphon the water into an ostrich egg. The depth to a sip well varies greatly, depending on the depth of the wet sands. Sometimes they are only one meter below the surface, but in dry times they can be as far as three meters from the surface.

tablier egyptien. A natural apron over the female Bushmen's genitals.

trekkers. Pioneers, white Europeans, mainly Boers or the Dutch, who landed in South Africa in the late 1600s and traveled north by ox-drawn wagon to settle and farm.

Tshjamm. Bushmen greeting.

veld. Grassland.

veldkos. Food gathered in the veld.

werf. A Bushman camp.

zhu dole. Dangerous person, such as the Bantu or European peoples.

zhu twa si. The name the !Kung Bushmen call themselves; literally the harmless people.

zo si. The Bushmen name for powerful peoples, such as the Bantu and Europeans; literally animals without hooves.

Bibliography

Books

Bannister, Anthony. *The Bushmen.* Cape Town, South Africa: Struik, 1984.

Barnard, Alan. *Kalahari Bushmen: Threatened Cultures.* New York: Thomson Learning, 1993.

Bleek, Dr. W. H. I. *Reynard the Fox in South Africa; or, Hottentot Fables and Tales.* London: Trubner, 1864.

____. *The Mantis and His Friends, Bushmen Folklore.* Collected by the late Dr. W. H. I. Bleek and the late Dr. Lucy C. Lloyd. Edited by D. F. Bleek. Illustrated with many reproductions of Bushmen drawings. Cape Town, South Africa: T. Maskew Miller, 1923.

Bowen, Elenore Smith (Laura Bohannan). *Return to Laughter.* Foreword by David Riesman. Published in cooperation with American Museum of Natural History. Garden City, NY: Natural History Library, Anchor Books, Doubleday, 1964.

Bulpin, T. V. *The Ivory Trail.* 2d ed. Johannesburg, South Africa: Books of Africa, in association with Southern Book Publishers, 1967.

Campbell, Joseph. *The Hero with a Thousand Faces.* Princeton, NJ: Princeton University Press, 1949.

Chatwin, Bruce. *The Songline.* New York: Viking Penguin, 1987.

Conrad, Joseph. *Heart of Darkness.* New York: Penguin Books, 1983.

Fourie, Coral. *Living Legends of a Dying Culture.* Hartbeespoort, South Africa: Ekogilde, 1994.

Helfman, Elizabeth S. *The Bushmen and Their Stories.* Drawings by Richard Cuffari. New York: Seabury Press, 1971.

Howard, Moses L. *The Ostrich Chase.* Illustrated by Barbara Seuling. New York: Holt, Rinehart and Winston, 1974.

Johnson, Peter, and Anthony Bannister. *The Bushmen.* Text by Alf Wannenburgh. Cape Town, South Africa: Struik, 1979.

Johnson, R. Townley. *Major Rock Paintings of Southern Africa: Facsimile Reproductions.* Cape Town, South Africa: David Philip, 1979.

Liebenberg, Louis. *The Art of Tracking: The Origin of Science.* Claremont, South Africa: David Philip, 1990.

Markowitz, Arthur. *The Rebirth of the Ostrich: And Other Stories of the Kalahari Bushmen Told in Their Manner.* Mafeking: Mafeking Mail, 1971.

Matthee, Dalene. *Circles in the Forest.* London: Penguin Books, 1985.

Morgan, Marlo. *Mutant Message Down Under.* Illustrated by Carri Garrison. New York: HarperCollins, 1994.

Plog, Fred, and Daniel G. Bates, with Joan Ross Acocella. *Dobe Kung Bushmen.* Cultural Anthropology. New York: Alfred A. Knopf, 1980.

Schapera, I. *The Khoisan Peoples of South Africa: Bushmen and Hottentots.* London: Routledge & Kegan Paul, 1930.

Thomas, Elizabeth Marshall. *The Harmless People: The Gikwe Bushmen.* New York: Vintage Books, 1958.

van der Post, Laurens. *A Far Off-Place.* New York: Harcourt Brace Jovanovich, 1974.

_____. *A Mantis Carol.* Washington, DC, Covelo, CA: Island Press, 1983.

_____. *A Walk with a White Bushman.* In conversation with Jean-Marc Pottiez. London: Chatto & Windus, 1986; New York: William Morrow, 1986.

_____. *Feather Fall: An Anthology.* Edited by Jean-Marc Pottiez. London: Chatto & Windus, 1994; New York: William Morrow, 1994.

_____. *Patterns of Renewal.* Wallingford, PA: Pendle Hill, 1962.

_____. *The Dark Eye of Africa.* New York: William Morrow, 1955.

_____. *The Heart of the Hunter.* Harmondsworth, Middlesex, England: Penguin Books in association with Hogarth Press, 1961.

_____. *The Lost World of the Kalahari.* New York: Harcourt Brace Jovanovich, 1958.

_____. *The Lost World of the Kalahari: With the Great and the Little Memory.* Photographs by David Coulson. Illustrated edition with a new epilogue by the author. London: Chatto & Windus, 1988.

____. *The Voice of the Thunder*. London: Chatto & Windus, 1993; New York: William Morrow, 1994.

Willcox, A. R., with a foreword by Professor J. Desmond Clark. *The Rock Art of South Africa*. Johannesberg, South Africa: Thomas Nelson & Sons, 1963.

Films

A Far Off-Place. Based on the books *A Story Like the Wind* and *A Far Off-Place* by Laurens van der Post. Screenplay by Robert Caswell, Jonathan Hensleigh and Sally Robinson. Produced by Eva Monley and Elaine Spencer. Directed by Mikael Salomon. Presented in association with Touchwood Pacific Partners. Amblin Entertainment. Walt Disney Home Video. 1995.

Eternal Enemies: Lions and Hyenas. Produced by Dereck Joubert and Beverly Joubert. Botswana: Wildlife Films, 1982.

Lost World of the Kalahari. By Laurens van der Post. The complete series: "The Nature of Exploration Today," "Vanishing People," "First Encounter," "The Spirit of the Slippery Hills," "Life in the Thirst Land," "The Great Eland," "The Rain Song." Films for the Humanities, 1954, 1993.

The Gods Must Be Crazy. Written and produced by Jamie Uys. Twentieth Century Fox Production, 1980.

The Gods Must Be Crazy, Part II. Written and produced by Jamie Uys. Columbia Pictures, 1990.

The Stolen River. Produced by Dereck Joubert and Beverly Joubert. Botswana: Wildlife Films, 1982.

Testament to the Bushmen. Laurens van der Post and South African BBC, 1984.

Audio Cassettes

Transformations of Myth Through Time. Joseph Campbell. "The Soul of the Ancients," "The Western Way," "The Wisdom of the East." St. Paul, MN: Highbridge Productions, 1990.

About the Author

I. Murphy Lewis resides in New York City and is currently the sales manager of Mary McFadden, Inc., a couture fashion house. In her spare time, she can be found traipsing across the Kalahari Desert in search of the dwindling Bushmen tribes or adding notes to her journal of 6,498 pages, which she's kept faithfully for the last 24 years.

Ms. Lewis is working on several documentaries about the Bushmen and their folklore for children and is writing another book about their god, *Mantis at Play*. In addition, she recently researched and republished a children's book, *Poems for Peter*, written by Lysbeth Boyd Borie in 1928, from the original copper plates (Shank Painter Publishing, 508-487-9169). She is presently co-authoring a book, *Lost Glamour: Rediscovering the Life of Lilly Dache*, a hat designer from 1924 to 1968, with Jeffrey Moss.

I. Murphy Lewis photographed with Izak Barnard.
(Photograph by Count Alexander von Roon.)

DATE DUE